What A
the Nev
Spirituality?

Booklets in the Searching Issues series:

Why Does God Allow Suffering?

What About Other Religions?

Is There a Conflict Between Science and Christianity?

What About the New Spirituality?

Does Religion Do More Harm Than Good?

Is the Trinity Unbiblical, Unbelievable and Irrelevant?

Is Faith Irrational?

What About the New Spirituality?

NICKY GUMBEL

Scripture quotations taken from
the Holy Bible, New International
Version Anglicised. Copyright ©
1979, 1984, 2011 Biblica, formerly
International Bible Society. Used by
permission of Hodder & Stoughton
Publishers, an Hachette UK
company. All rights reserved. 'NIV'
is a registered trademark of Biblica.
UK trademark number 1448790.

Published by Alpha International
HTB Brompton Road
London SW7 1JA
Email: publications@alpha.org
Website: alpha.org
@alphacourse

Illustrated by Charlie Mackesy

Contents

Contents

What About the New Spirituality?

A quick trip to the 'Mind, Body, Spirit' shelf of most bookshops or to the 'Religion and Spirituality' section of online retailers reveals a bewildering range of contemporary answers to questions about who we are, about how we can change and live more meaningful lives, and about God or the divine.

Some approach these questions in an eclectic way, pulling together words of wisdom and the sentiments of respected thinkers from a variety of religious traditions (or none) down through the ages, offering people whichever perspectives and answers best resonate with their lives.

Others invite people to commit themselves to a particular path, whether that of the 'New Age', of a particular pop psychology or form of self-help, or of ideas taken from Buddhism and eastern spiritualities. Some of these ideas are quite new, while others are older ideas and movements that are regaining popularity. Together they make up what we might group under the broad heading 'the new spirituality'.

Statistics suggest that more than 92 million books were sold in the 'Mind, Body, Spirit' category in the US in 1999, around 9 per cent of total book sales. Of those, 34 per cent were inspirational titles, 28 per cent diet related, 16 per cent psychology and 13 per cent New Age. Rhonda Byrne's *The Secret*, a manifesto for 'positive thinking' published in 2006, remained at the top of *The New York Times* Best Seller list for 146 consecutive weeks. Eckhart Tolle's recent book *The Power of Now: A Guide to Spiritual Enlightenment* spent 1,986 days in Amazon's Top 100.

All this provides yet another indicator that people everywhere are thinking about ways in which there might be *more* to life. In a 2005 Europe-wide survey, 74 per cent of people answered that they think about the meaning of life either 'sometimes' or 'often', while over two-thirds of the group who said 'yes' to that question also answered that they believe not in a 'conventional' God but rather in some sort of spirit or life force.[1] Meanwhile, in the USA, the number of people who identified themselves as 'pagan' more than doubled between 2001 and 2008, while those identifying themselves as 'spiritualist' shot up from 116,000 to 420,000.[2]

My perspective as a Christian living in the Western world is that we live in extraordinary and changing times. We are living in the midst of a revolution in the way we think and the way in which we look at the world. At the same time as a scientific worldview is beginning to enter popular consciousness more deeply, the restrictiveness of what we could call the Enlightenment worldview and framework is also being questioned by many.

In pre-Enlightenment times, reason was viewed as a tool of understanding but was subordinated to the revealed truth of Christianity, which was seen as thoroughly supernatural. The seventeenth and eighteenth centuries saw a shift in the European way of thinking that is now broadly defined as the Enlightenment. Reason, which had previously been considered a useful tool, was now celebrated as the power by which we can understand the universe and improve the human condition. The Enlightenment brought enormous progress in science, technology and medicine, but within it were the seeds of its own destruction. Revelation was made subject to reason.

This turn-around was to have a huge effect on people's response to Christianity. However, most ordinary people in the eighteenth century were largely unaffected by such philosophical wranglings. The secularisation of Western society began in earnest throughout the nineteenth century, although the Victorian era was still powerfully influenced by Christian ideas.

Then, in the twentieth century, the full implications of the Enlightenment started to be seen. Since revelation was subject to reason, the miracles of Scripture, and indeed the traditional concept of God, began to be explained rationally. The faith of a society was being eroded. The fruits of the seeds sown in earlier centuries were seen in a devastatingly clear light.

Now, in our own day, many are questioning the suppositions of the Enlightenment. We can no longer be described as a secular society – we live in an age that is the most religious for several generations. It is also an age of 'new spirituality'. Rising up out of this shift of thinking, many are resisting rationalism. It has highlighted well the emptiness and shortcomings of rationalism and materialism. The 'new spirituality' emphasises experience and values spirituality, but it goes further than this.

What is the new spirituality?

Bishop Graham Cray has described Western culture as a 'pick-and-mix culture'. What we have called 'new spirituality' is an umbrella term that covers various diverse and disparate movements with a seemingly limitless array of disconnected beliefs and lifestyles. Sometimes people are committed to a particular path, while at other times it is more a matter of dabbling in whatever works for a certain individual. It is almost impossible to define because it has so many different branches. It has no leader, no organisation, no structure and no headquarters. It is a groundswell, an uncentralised movement of many diverse constituents. Caryl Matrisciana, looking back on her experience of many years involved in the New Age movement, for example, describes it as being like the recipe for a cake:

> 2 cups of hope (carefully sift out all fear)
> 2 cups of altered consciousness (Yoga, drugs, or meditation to taste)
> 3 tablespoons each of self-awareness, self-improvement and self-esteem (be sure to melt away anything negative)
> 1 heaped teaspoon of peace
> 1 large dollop of love
> 1 generous pinch each of humanism, Eastern mysticism and occultism

1 handful of holism
1 scoop of mystical experience.
Mix thoroughly together. Bake in a warm,
friendly environment. Fill with your most
appealing dreams. Garnish generously with
positive thoughts and good vibrations.[3]

On the surface, parts of this new spirituality are either good or harmless. It often comes in the guise of self-help programmes, holistic health, a concern for world peace, ecology and spiritual enlightenment. Indeed, by themselves, certain elements such as the stress on good nutrition, the avoidance of drugs and respect for creation find an ally in Christianity. However, often under the sugar coating there is a dangerous pill. As St Paul warns us, 'Satan himself masquerades as an angel of light' (2 Corinthians 11:14).

First, it is often a mixture of Eastern mysticism and other practices that have been given a Western materialistic flavour.

Hindu and Buddhist doctrines have been adapted for the Western world. A string of gurus has blended Eastern concepts with a Western thirst for fulfilment, expression and enlightenment. There is a great deal of teaching on karma and Zen.

Second, there is the influence of nature religions from around the world, including the folk beliefs of American Indians and Wicca witchcraft.

Third, there are a number of practices that are overtly occult in nature. Astrology, horoscopes, fortune-telling, clairvoyance, consulting the dead, spiritism, mediums, channelling, spirit guides and tarot cards are all widely used. All practices such as these are condemned in the Bible: 'Let no one be found among you who sacrifices his son or daughter in the fire, who practises divination or sorcery, interprets omens, engages in witchcraft, or casts spells, or who is a medium or spiritist or who consults the dead. Anyone who does these things is detestable to the Lord' (Deuteronomy 18:10–12). These warnings are reiterated elsewhere in the Bible (Leviticus 19:26, 31; Galatians 5:20; Revelation 9:20–21).

The influence of the movement has been very significant, sometimes in particular within celebrity culture. Among many other movements, Kabbalah is a current fascination of many. Eitan Yardeni, who has given one-on-one instruction to Madonna, Demi Moore, and Roseanne Barr, suggested in an interview that such practices help celebrities deal with stardom:

> The rule in Kabbalah is that the more a person has, the more they need to work on themselves, in every area... With that power of having so much comes a greater challenge, a great amount of work to become humble about it. It's a struggle, to have so much...

With celebrities, at least those who are honest with themselves and ready to do the spiritual work, they realise that fame is not enough. The test is to realise that the temporary glitz, the temporary high, the temporary fame, is not true power. If you let the power control you, you'll be miserable. That's just the truth.[4]

What are the beliefs of 'new spirituality'?

The 'new spirituality' is both diverse and disparate, making it hard to summarise its beliefs. Generally, however, the ideals include being connected to the energy of creation, but spirituality doesn't necessarily mean having a religious context. Spirituality is seen as being what and who people are. These strands of thought illustrate a vision of the world which late theologian John Stott describes in what he calls 'three pithy sayings': 'All is God', 'All is one' and 'All is well'.[5]

The first, 'All is God', is generally known as pantheism. God is in everything. He is de-personified. He is an impersonal energy, a creative force. A god-like force runs through all creation: trees, animals, rocks and people. In many strands of thinking in 'new spirituality', there is no distinction between the creator and what he has created. The earth is divine, as are the stars and planets. This sometimes leads to a return to the pagan worship of Mother Earth and to the belief that the stars and planets and even crystals have power and influence.

In the New Age movement, there is no God outside his creation. God lies within each of us, and we are each a part of God. Actress and prominent New Age advocate Shirley MacLaine states that 'Everyone is God. Everyone.' Similarly, Eckhart Tolle writes:

> Identification with your mind creates an opaque screen of concepts, labels, images, words, judgments, and definitions that blocks all true relationship. It comes between you and yourself, between you and your fellow man and woman, between you and nature, between you and God. It is this screen of thought that creates the illusion of separateness, the illusion that there is you and a totally separate 'other.' You then forget the essential fact that, underneath the level of physical appearances and separate forms, you are one with all that is.[6]

The way to find God is to look within. Hence the title of one of Shirley MacLaine's books is *Going Within*. Swami Muktananda says, 'Kneel to your own self. Honour and worship your own being. God dwells within you as you.' In a UK television interview with Michael Parkinson, the British novelist and comedy scriptwriter Ben Elton commented, 'I think it's fairly well accepted that we live in a post-faith age... but people still need faith and they find it in all sorts of ways. God famously made man in his image but now I think we make God in man's image. People choose a religion: "the God of my choice".'

Choosing our own God like this can seem very attractive, but ultimately it cannot fulfil the 'need' that Elton speaks about. G. K. Chesterton highlighted the problems in 1908 in his book *Orthodoxy*: 'Of all conceivable forms of enlightenment the worst is what... people call the inner-light. Of all horrible religions the most horrible is the god within. That Jones shall worship the God within him turns out ultimately to mean that Jones shall worship Jones.' Humankind has fallen once again for the primeval temptation: 'you will be like God' (Genesis 3:5).

Although there is a great deal of talk about compassion and love, the 'new spirituality' movement is often self-centred. The starting point for change (with perhaps the long-term goal of helping others) is the development of the self. The worship of self manifests itself in books and courses on self-realisation, self-fulfilment, self-help, self-confidence, self-improvement, self-worth, self-esteem and self-love. The highest goal is to find one's own happiness, satisfaction and success. To find one's own self is to find God.

This, of course, is an explicit assault on the self-denial at the heart of true Christianity. It is the opposite of the New Testament, where the way of fulfilment is loving and serving a personal God and loving and serving others. The way of fulfilment is not self-worship but self-denial, exemplified supremely in the life, death and resurrection of Jesus Christ.

Second, 'All is one', for which the technical term is 'monism'. The new spirituality is essentially syncretistic. It attempts to reconcile opposites and bring about a synthesis of all religions. In so doing, it rejects much orthodox Christianity, which is seen as rigid, structured and blinkered.

Moral absolutes are often rejected: 'sin' is not a popular word in the new spirituality, which thinks that our problem is not sin, but ignorance of our true self and true potential. This is solved by enlightenment, spiritual revelation and education. For some, there is no objective standard of right and wrong. As one spiritual sage from India put it, when speaking to Caryl Matrisciana, 'It's not a question of whether you are good or bad... good and bad are relative. They are two sides of one coin, part of the same whole.'[7]

In a similar vein, Carl Frederick wrote in *est: Playing the Game the New Way*, 'You are the Supreme being... there isn't any right or wrong.' Shirley MacLaine's philosophy might be summed up as: 'If it feels good, do it.' The New Age offers the attraction of a spirituality without the cost of repentance. It is sometimes called 'hippy values for a modern lifestyle'.

Guidance comes from within. John W. Travis and Regina Sara Ryan in the *Wellness Workbook* write:

> So if love is as natural as breathing, and eating, and working and playing, it is as natural as 'sexing'. If love becomes our 'life support system,' then every decision we make, sex included, will be guided by it. We will choose to have sex with one another if it enhances our experience of unification with all that is.[8]

Since our problem is not sin but ignorance, there can be no judgment. In contrast to the Christian view that 'people are destined to die once, and after that to face judgment' (Hebrews 9:27), some subscribe to a belief in reincarnation. Reincarnation is not always taught as cosmic justice, where we will be graded up or down depending on how good or bad we have been. Rather, everyone is eventually making progress onwards and upwards towards complete spiritual enlightenment and perfection. Again, they have fallen for Satan's lie: 'You will not surely die' (Genesis 3:4).

Monism ('All is one') is taken to even further extremes in some parts of the spirituality, in which there is no distinction made between God and Satan. Since all is one, the devil himself is worshipped.

The third saying with which John Stott summarises the new spirituality is 'All is well'. Under this heading we can group the many and varied hopes new spiritualities offer for a better life and a better future for the world. The solution to many of the world's most complex problems are said to be 'spiritual' solutions. As comedian and author Russell Brand wrote in *The Guardian* following the British riots of 2011:

> Young people have no sense of community because they haven't been given one. They have no stake in society... I don't know enough about politics to ponder a solution and my hands are sticky with blood money from representing corporate interests through film, television and commercials, venerating, through my endorsements and celebrity, products and a lifestyle that contributes to the alienation of

an increasingly dissatisfied underclass. But I
know, as we all intuitively know, the solution is
all around us and it isn't political, it is spiritual.
Gandhi said: 'Be the change you want to see
in the world.'[9]

Once again, Christians can find an ally in this hope for
a 'spiritual' change in the most difficult issues facing
societies today, but for very different reasons. For some
this hope is incredibly expansive, and involves a new
world order and a new world religion.

Jesus warned against such claims:

For false Christs and false prophets will appear
and perform great signs and miracles to
deceive even the elect – if that were possible.
See, I have told you ahead of time.

So if anyone tells you, 'There he is, out in
the desert,' do not go out; or, 'Here he is, in the
inner rooms,' do not believe it. For as lightning
that comes from the east is visible even in the
west, so will be the coming of the Son of Man.
Matthew 24:24–27

What is wrong with the new spirituality?
The new spirituality is right to challenge the prevailing
materialism and rationalism of our times. It is right to

emphasise the importance of experience and to value spirituality. It is right to stress compassion, love and unity. Millions who are engaged in the new spirituality are on the right track in the sense that they are searching for spiritual reality. Yet these emphases fall way short of the glorious truths of Christianity.

We in the church are often to blame for having presented a form of Christianity that is hierarchical, structured and narrow-minded. We can sympathise with David Icke when he wrote, 'I feel the traditional Church as an organisation has let down the world badly with its dogma and rigidity'[10] and with Oprah Winfrey when she writes of religion that is just doctrine without spirituality.[11]

The remedy lies not in the rejection of Christianity, but in a reappraisal of what is at the heart of the Christian faith. When we look at this, we see how far short the new spirituality movement falls of the glorious truth about the Trinitarian God of the orthodox Christian faith.

First, it does not get near the truth about God the Father. God is not an impersonal, abstract force, but the transcendent personal creator of the whole universe. And yet he is immanent. He wants to be in a relationship with us as human beings. We can speak to him and he speaks to us. He is a Father who loves us and we are called to respond in love to him and for our brothers and sisters. These are the glorious truths on which our Christian culture is built. The new spirituality will take us back to paganism, and St Paul warns us against those who 'exchanged the truth of God for a lie, and worshipped and served created things rather than the Creator' (Romans 1:25).

We were made to live in a relationship that involves the love and worship of God. As St Augustine put it, 'You have made us for yourself, and our heart is restless until it rests in you.'[12] That is why there is a restlessness within the new spirituality. There is a continual searching for an illusory peace. Shirley MacLaine writes: 'Whenever I ask people what they want for themselves and for the world, the answer is almost always the same – peace.'[13]

Sadly, this continual search can easily go awry. One woman in our congregation who was involved in the New Age for about three years told me about her initial feeling of self-growth, and being set to 'break the rules'. But soon she found she was imprisoned.

> I was like a lamb to the slaughter. It was like being on drugs. I was constantly looking for bigger experiences. I went on more and more expensive courses. I felt I was going out of my mind. It leaves you stuck in a place you don't understand – where you can't relate to the

> world. It led me away from anything good and
> nourishing. You just don't know when you are
> going to be healed.

She eventually found fulfilment, peace and healing in a relationship with God the Father, who alone can bring true and lasting peace.

Second, the new spirituality does not get near the truth about God the Son. Jesus is seen as one of the ascended masters, along with Buddha, Krishna and others. Extraordinary rewritings of the New Testament Gospel accounts abound. Shirley MacLaine has even claimed that Jesus was a member of the Essenes, whose 'teachings, principles, values and priorities in life were so similar to those of the so-called New Age today... Christ demonstrated what we would today call precognition... levitation, telepathy and occult healing.'[14]

David Icke claims that between the ages of twelve and thirty 'Jesus travelled widely to countries like India, Greece, Turkey, Egypt, France and England... He once had to self-heal himself after contracting tuberculosis.' According to Icke, his disciples were 'all Planetary Devas'. After his death on the cross 'friends buried the body in a cellar and it has never been found'.[15] However ingenious these suggestions might be, there is absolutely no historical evidence to support any of them.

At the most extreme end, the Bhagwan Shree Rajneesh bought a town in America and set up his own Ashram where his Western disciples underwent enlightenment therapy, which put emphasis on sex, drugs and violence. The net gain to the Bhagwan was a garage full of ninety-three Rolls Royces. Jesus was rich, but for our sakes became poor so that we might become rich. The Bhagwan was poor, but became rich and in doing so left a lot of others very poor.

In trying to accommodate Jesus into the new spirituality, adherents miss out on the glorious truth of Jesus Christ, that he is 'the way and the truth and the life' (John 14:6). He was, and is, God made man for our salvation. In his great love, Jesus died on the cross for us, in order to free us from guilt, addiction, fear and death. He made forgiveness possible, bringing us friendship with God, the experience of his love and the power to change.

Consequently, he liberates us to love and serve others and to become more like Jesus himself. These things are at the heart of the biblical understanding of salvation. This salvation is not something we could ever earn or achieve ourselves; it is a free gift from God. The only salvation in the new spirituality is self-salvation and the only forgiveness is self-forgiveness. In *A Course in Miracles*,[16] a typical workbook used by many in the New Age movement for daily reading, lesson 70 is headed 'My salvation comes from me.' The reader is urged to repeat, 'My salvation comes from me. It cannot come from anywhere else.' On the contrary, the New Testament asserts that Jesus is the only way of salvation (Acts 4:12). The new spirituality misses out on this wonderful news.

It misses out too on the good news of his resurrection British church leader Michael Green writes:

> Our destiny is not to go through many purgative reincarnations until the grossness of our lives is melted away, but after death to share in the resurrection life of which the Easter Jesus is the pledge. 'To depart is to be with Christ, which is far better.'
>
> 'We shall be like him, when we see him as he is.' That is the conviction of those who knew him. Is it beyond belief? Not reincarnation, based on karma, but resurrection, based on the cross and resurrection of Jesus, which points both to our forgiveness and to our destiny. A totally different world view. And one which challenges us to make up our minds, and choose.[17]

Third, new spirituality does not get near the truth about God the Holy Spirit. In the new spirituality we see a search for spiritual power, spiritual experience and transformed lives. There is no greater spiritual power than the power of the Holy Spirit, no greater experience than the fullness of the Holy Spirit and no more effective power to transform our lives.

One woman told me how she had tried Buddhism, Zen, Hinduism, transcendental meditation, the occult and all kinds of other practices. Then one day she read Jackie Pullinger's book *Chasing the Dragon*, about her work among drug addicts in Hong Kong. She went out there and saw people being set free and healed by the power of the Holy Spirit. She saw the life, love, joy and peace the Holy Spirit brought to people's lives. I asked her what the difference was between that and her experiences in the New Age. She replied that she had seen real power in both, but added, 'One power, the New Age power, meant opting out of society, whereas the power of the Holy Spirit meant opting back into society and changing people's lives.'

It is interesting that at a time of great outpouring of the power and gifts of the Holy Spirit in the worldwide church (which began at the turn of the century) we are seeing what appears to be a satanic counterfeit (which began shortly afterwards). But Satan cannot counterfeit holiness. The Holy Spirit transforms Christians into the likeness of Jesus Christ (2 Corinthians 3:18). The fruit of the Spirit is love, joy, peace, patience, kindness, goodness, faithfulness, gentleness and self-control (Galatians 5:22–23).

What are we to do?

First, there is a need for a double repentance. On the one hand, if we have been involved in any way in practices of the new spirituality, whether unwittingly or not, we need to recognise that they are wrong and to ask God's forgiveness and turn away from all such things. We need to turn to Jesus Christ who died on the cross so that we could be forgiven. We need to ask the Holy Spirit to come and live within us.

On the other hand, those of us who have been involved in the church need to repent of our rigidity, rationalism and failure to make the church relevant to the culture in which we live. We should also acknowledge where new spirituality has properly challenged our own prejudices. The interest in holistic medicine, for example, does in some senses move us back towards a true Christian understanding of the human being as one, rather than making a distinction between body and soul.

Second, we need to soak ourselves in the truth. Paul warns us: 'See to it that no one takes you captive through hollow and deceptive philosophy' (Colossians 2:8) and again in Timothy:

> For the time will come when people will not put up with sound doctrine. Instead, to suit their own desires, they will gather around them a great number of teachers to say what their itching

ears want to hear. They will turn their ears away
from the truth and turn aside to myths. But you,
keep your head in all situations.
2 Timothy 4:3–5

We don't need to read lots of books about new
spirituality. The way to spot a counterfeit is to know
the real thing really well. Caryl Matrisciana uses a
helpful analogy:

'Mum's been working at the bank for over a
year,' my friend Chris told me. 'And she's been
getting the most amazing education.'

'What do you mean?'

'She's learning all about money.'

'I guess she'd have to know about money if
she's going to work in a bank!' I laughed.

Chris smiled. 'I mean she's really learning
about money. They are teaching her to know the
colour of each bill, the size of it, even the way it's
water marked. They are showing her the details
of the inks and papers.'

'How do they teach her?'

'Well, they just keep having her handle it.
They point out all the various things they want
her to remember. But they figure the more she
works with money, feels it, counts it, and stacks
it, the more familiar it'll be to her.'

'That makes sense, I suppose. But what's the point?'

'Here's the point. Yesterday they blindfolded her. They slipped a couple of counterfeit bills in her stack of money. She picked them out by touch!'

'So she's studying counterfeit money too, then?'

'No… that's just it. The people at the bank know that a person doesn't need to study the counterfeits.'

'I see. But it seems as if they're going to a lot of trouble, doesn't it?'

'Not really. The banks know that the counterfeits are getting better and better, more and more sophisticated. And it's been proved a thousand times over that *if a bank teller knows the real money extremely well, he can't be fooled by the counterfeits.*'[18]

Third, we need to bring the good news of Jesus to those who are involved in the new spirituality. On the whole, those involved are simply people searching for the truth. They recognise that materialism does not satisfy. They recognise the limits of reason. They are seeking an experience of the spiritual. We need to demonstrate by our lives the supernatural power of God: Father, Son and Holy Spirit.

Endnotes

1. European Commission, Social Values, Science and Technology Report, 2005: http://ec.europa.eu/public_ opinion/archives/ebs/ebs_225_report_en.pdf

2. Statistics from the US Census 2008: http://www. census.gov/compendia/statab/2012/tables/12s0075. pdf

3. Caryl Matrisciana, Gods of the New Age (Marshall Pickering, 1985), p.15.

4. New York Mag, 'Our Lady of Malawi', 1 May 2011: http://nymag.com/print/?/news/features/ madonna-malawi-2011-5/

5. John Stott, 'Conflicting Gospels', CEN (8 December 1989), p.6.

6. Eckhart Tolle, The Power of Now: A Guide to Spiritual Enlightenment (Hodder, 2001).

7. Caryl Matrisciana, op cit, p.81.

8. John W. Travis and Regina Sara Ryan, Wellness Workbook, 3rd edition (Ten Speed Press, 2004), p.258.

9. Russell Brand, The Guardian, 'Big Brother isn't watching you', 11 August 2011.

10. David Icke, The Truth Vibrations (The Aquarian Press, HarperCollins, 1991), p.20.

11. See http://www.oprah.com/omagazine/A-New- Earth-What-I-Know-for-Sure-by-Oprah-Winfrey

12. St Augustine, Confessions, Book 1, Section 1.

13. Shirley Maclaine, Going Within (Bantam Press, 1989), p.30.

14. Ibid., pp.180–81.

15. David Icke, op cit, pp.115–17.

16. Foundation for Inner Peace, A Course in Miracles (Penguin, 1975).

17. Michael Green, The Dawn of the New Age (Darton, Longman & Todd Ltd, 1993), p.86.

18. Caryl Matrisciana, op cit, p.220.

Alpha

Alpha is a practical introduction to the Christian faith, initiated by HTB in London and now being run by thousands of churches, of many denominations, throughout the world. If you are interested in finding out more about the Christian faith and would like details of your nearest Alpha, please visit our website:

alpha.org

or contact:
The Alpha Office,
HTB Brompton Road,
London,
SW7 1JA

Tel: 0845 644 7544

About the Author

Nicky Gumbel is the pioneer of Alpha. He read law at Cambridge and theology at Oxford, practised as a barrister and is now vicar of HTB in London. He is the author of many bestselling books about the Christian faith, including *Questions of Life*, *The Jesus Lifestyle*, *Why Jesus?*, *A Life Worth Living*, *Searching Issues* and *30 Days*.